EMMANUEL JOSEPH

Global Tech Pioneers, Unveiling Future Innovations in Business and Beyond

Copyright © 2025 by Emmanuel Joseph

All rights reserved. No part of this publication may be reproduced, stored or transmitted in any form or by any means, electronic, mechanical, photocopying, recording, scanning, or otherwise without written permission from the publisher. It is illegal to copy this book, post it to a website, or distribute it by any other means without permission.

First edition

This book was professionally typeset on Reedsy.
Find out more at reedsy.com

Contents

1. Chapter 1: The Dawn of a New Era — 1
2. Chapter 2: Artificial Intelligence and Machine Learning — 3
3. Chapter 3: The Internet of Things: Connecting Everything — 5
4. Chapter 4: Blockchain: Beyond Cryptocurrency — 6
5. Chapter 5: The Rise of Automation and Robotics — 8
6. Chapter 6: Big Data and Analytics: Harnessing the Power of... — 10
7. Chapter 7: Cybersecurity: Protecting the Digital Frontier — 12
8. Chapter 8: The Future of Work: Embracing Digital... — 14
9. Chapter 9: Sustainability and Green Technology — 15
10. Chapter 10: HealthTech: Revolutionizing Healthcare — 17
11. Chapter 11: FinTech: Redefining Financial Services — 19
12. Chapter 12: EdTech: Transforming Education — 21
13. Chapter 13: The Role of Government and Policy in Tech... — 22
14. Chapter 14: Ethical Considerations in Technology — 24
15. Chapter 15: The Road Ahead: Embracing Innovation for a... — 26

1

Chapter 1: The Dawn of a New Era

The world stands on the precipice of a technological revolution, where the lines between the physical and digital realms blur into a seamless tapestry of innovation. This new era is defined by rapid advancements in technology, reshaping industries, economies, and societies at an unprecedented pace. The transformative potential of cutting-edge technologies like artificial intelligence (AI), blockchain, and the Internet of Things (IoT) is undeniable, driving businesses to rethink their strategies and embrace the future.

Visionary leaders are at the forefront of this revolution, harnessing the power of technology to drive change and create value. From Silicon Valley to Shenzhen, these pioneers are pushing the boundaries of what's possible, setting the stage for a future where technology is not just a tool, but a fundamental enabler of progress. Through their stories and achievements, we gain insight into the forces shaping our world and the limitless possibilities that lie ahead.

In this chapter, we explore the dawn of this new era, examining the key drivers of technological change and their implications for businesses and society. We'll delve into real-world examples of companies that have successfully navigated the digital transformation journey, highlighting the strategies and mindsets that have propelled them to the forefront of innovation. By understanding the foundations of this revolution, we can better appreciate the transformative power of technology and its potential to redefine our future.

2

Chapter 2: Artificial Intelligence and Machine Learning

Artificial intelligence (AI) and machine learning (ML) are revolutionizing the way we interact with technology, enabling machines to learn from data, adapt to new information, and perform tasks that were once the exclusive domain of humans. These technologies are transforming industries across the board, from healthcare to finance, and unlocking new levels of efficiency, accuracy, and personalization.

At the heart of AI and ML is the ability to process vast amounts of data and extract meaningful insights. Through advanced algorithms and computational power, machines can now analyze patterns, make predictions, and optimize processes in ways that were previously unimaginable. This chapter delves into the mechanics of AI and ML, exploring the fundamental principles that underpin these technologies and their real-world applications.

We will examine how AI and ML are enhancing decision-making, from predicting customer preferences to optimizing supply chains. In healthcare, AI-powered diagnostic tools are revolutionizing patient care, enabling early detection of diseases and personalized treatment plans. In finance, machine learning algorithms are driving innovation in fraud detection, investment strategies, and risk management.

By understanding the transformative potential of AI and ML, businesses can leverage these technologies to gain a competitive edge and drive innovation. This chapter provides a comprehensive overview of the key concepts, applications, and benefits of AI and ML, offering valuable insights for businesses looking to embrace the future.

3

Chapter 3: The Internet of Things: Connecting Everything

The Internet of Things (IoT) is creating a world where everything is connected, from household appliances to industrial machinery, generating a continuous stream of data that drives intelligent decision-making. This network of interconnected devices is revolutionizing industries by enabling real-time monitoring, predictive maintenance, and automated processes.

IoT technology is transforming cities into smart cities, where sensors and data analytics optimize traffic flow, energy consumption, and public services. In agriculture, IoT-enabled devices are enhancing crop management, improving yields, and reducing resource usage. In manufacturing, IoT is enabling predictive maintenance, minimizing downtime, and optimizing production processes.

This chapter explores the IoT landscape, highlighting the key components, applications, and benefits of this transformative technology. We will delve into real-world examples of IoT implementations, showcasing how businesses are leveraging connected devices to drive efficiencies, reduce costs, and innovate. By connecting the physical and digital worlds, IoT is creating new opportunities for businesses to thrive in an increasingly connected world.

4

Chapter 4: Blockchain: Beyond Cryptocurrency

Blockchain technology is often associated with cryptocurrencies like Bitcoin, but its potential extends far beyond digital currency. At its core, blockchain is a decentralized, transparent, and secure ledger system that has the potential to revolutionize industries by providing trust and transparency in transactions.

This chapter delves into the foundational principles of blockchain technology, exploring how it works and its potential applications. From supply chain management to intellectual property protection, blockchain is being adopted across various sectors to enhance security, efficiency, and trust.

In supply chain management, blockchain enables end-to-end visibility and traceability, ensuring the integrity of products and reducing the risk of fraud. In voting systems, blockchain provides a tamper-proof platform for secure and transparent elections. In intellectual property protection, blockchain allows creators to secure and manage their digital assets, ensuring fair compensation and reducing piracy.

By understanding the potential of blockchain technology, businesses can explore new opportunities for innovation and disruption. This chapter provides a comprehensive overview of the key concepts, applications, and benefits of blockchain, offering valuable insights for businesses looking to

CHAPTER 4: BLOCKCHAIN: BEYOND CRYPTOCURRENCY

embrace this transformative technology.

5

Chapter 5: The Rise of Automation and Robotics

Automation and robotics are no longer confined to the realm of science fiction; they are transforming industries and redefining the future of work. From assembly lines to autonomous vehicles, these technologies are enhancing productivity, efficiency, and precision. Automation involves the use of technology to perform tasks that were once carried out by humans, while robotics focuses on the development of machines that can perform complex actions autonomously.

In manufacturing, robotics is revolutionizing production processes, enabling companies to achieve higher output with lower costs. Collaborative robots, or cobots, are designed to work alongside humans, enhancing capabilities and ensuring safety. Autonomous vehicles are poised to transform transportation, reducing accidents and improving mobility.

The integration of automation and robotics extends beyond manufacturing and transportation. In healthcare, robotic surgery is enabling minimally invasive procedures, reducing recovery times and improving patient outcomes. In agriculture, automated systems are optimizing crop management and enhancing productivity. This chapter explores the latest advancements in automation and robotics, highlighting their applications and implications for various industries.

CHAPTER 5: THE RISE OF AUTOMATION AND ROBOTICS

By embracing automation and robotics, businesses can drive innovation, improve efficiency, and stay competitive in an ever-changing landscape. This chapter provides a comprehensive overview of the key concepts, applications, and benefits of these transformative technologies, offering valuable insights for businesses looking to harness their potential.

6

Chapter 6: Big Data and Analytics: Harnessing the Power of Information

In the digital age, data is a valuable asset that drives informed decision-making and fuels innovation. Big data refers to the vast amounts of structured and unstructured data generated by businesses and individuals daily. Analytics involves the use of advanced tools and techniques to collect, analyze, and interpret this data, transforming it into actionable intelligence.

This chapter delves into the world of big data and analytics, exploring how businesses leverage data to gain insights, optimize operations, and drive growth. By analyzing customer behavior, market trends, and operational performance, companies can make data-driven decisions that enhance competitiveness and improve outcomes.

In retail, big data analytics enables personalized marketing, optimizing inventory management, and enhancing customer experiences. In finance, data analytics drives fraud detection, risk management, and investment strategies. In healthcare, data-driven insights improve patient care, enhance diagnostics, and streamline processes.

By harnessing the power of big data and analytics, businesses can unlock new opportunities for innovation and growth. This chapter provides a comprehensive overview of the tools, techniques, and benefits of big data and analytics, offering valuable insights for businesses looking to leverage data for a competitive edge.

7

Chapter 7: Cybersecurity: Protecting the Digital Frontier

As technology advances, so do the threats to our digital infrastructure. Cybersecurity is the practice of protecting systems, networks, and data from cyber threats, ensuring the confidentiality, integrity, and availability of information. In an increasingly connected world, cybersecurity is critical for safeguarding sensitive information and ensuring business continuity.

This chapter focuses on the importance of cybersecurity, highlighting the latest trends and best practices for protecting digital assets. From threat detection to response strategies, businesses must stay vigilant and proactive in addressing cyber threats. Cyberattacks, such as ransomware, phishing, and data breaches, pose significant risks to organizations, and effective cybersecurity measures are essential to mitigate these threats.

In addition to technological solutions, cybersecurity requires a holistic approach that includes employee training, robust policies, and incident response plans. By fostering a culture of security awareness and implementing comprehensive cybersecurity strategies, businesses can protect their digital assets and maintain trust with customers and stakeholders.

This chapter provides a comprehensive overview of the key concepts, trends, and best practices in cybersecurity, offering valuable insights for businesses looking to enhance their security posture and protect their digital frontier.

8

Chapter 8: The Future of Work: Embracing Digital Transformation

Digital transformation is reshaping the workplace, enabling remote work, fostering collaboration, and enhancing productivity through digital tools. The future of work is defined by flexibility, agility, and continuous learning, as businesses adapt to new modes of operation and embrace technological advancements.

This chapter explores the future of work, examining how digital transformation is driving change and creating new opportunities for businesses and employees. Remote work, once considered a niche option, has become mainstream, enabled by digital tools that facilitate communication, collaboration, and project management. Businesses are leveraging cloud computing, artificial intelligence, and data analytics to enhance productivity and make informed decisions.

Digital transformation is also redefining employee engagement and organizational culture. Companies are adopting agile methodologies, promoting continuous learning, and fostering a culture of innovation. By embracing digital transformation, businesses can attract and retain top talent, enhance employee satisfaction, and drive growth.

9

Chapter 9: Sustainability and Green Technology

Sustainability has moved beyond a buzzword to become a pivotal consideration in modern business strategies. As global awareness of environmental issues grows, companies are increasingly turning to green technologies to reduce their carbon footprint and promote sustainable practices. This chapter delves into the innovative solutions that merge technology and sustainability, highlighting their impact on industries and society.

Renewable energy sources such as solar, wind, and hydro power are leading the charge in the transition to a greener future. Companies are investing in clean energy projects to reduce their dependence on fossil fuels and minimize greenhouse gas emissions. Green manufacturing processes, which prioritize energy efficiency and waste reduction, are revolutionizing the production of goods.

Beyond energy, the circular economy model is gaining traction, emphasizing the importance of reusing, recycling, and repurposing materials. This approach not only reduces waste but also creates new business opportunities and promotes resource efficiency. From sustainable packaging to eco-friendly transportation solutions, businesses are adopting green technologies to align with environmental goals and meet the growing demands of environmentally conscious consumers.

This chapter explores the intersection of technology and sustainability, showcasing real-world examples of businesses that have successfully integrated green practices into their operations. By embracing sustainability and green technology, companies can contribute to a healthier planet while driving innovation and competitiveness.

10

Chapter 10: HealthTech: Revolutionizing Healthcare

Technological advancements are transforming the healthcare landscape, offering new ways to diagnose, treat, and monitor patients. HealthTech, or healthcare technology, is revolutionizing the delivery of medical services, improving patient outcomes, and enhancing the overall healthcare experience.

Telemedicine, which enables remote consultations and virtual healthcare visits, has become increasingly popular, especially in underserved areas. Wearable devices, such as fitness trackers and smartwatches, allow individuals to monitor their health in real-time, providing valuable data for personalized healthcare.

Artificial intelligence (AI) and machine learning (ML) are driving innovation in diagnostics and treatment. AI-powered algorithms can analyze medical images with remarkable accuracy, aiding in the early detection of diseases such as cancer. Machine learning models are being used to develop personalized treatment plans based on a patient's unique genetic makeup and medical history.

In addition to improving patient care, HealthTech is streamlining administrative processes, reducing costs, and enhancing the efficiency of healthcare systems. Electronic health records (EHRs) provide a centralized repository of patient information, facilitating seamless communication and collaboration among healthcare providers.

This chapter explores the latest innovations in HealthTech, highlighting their applications and benefits. By leveraging technology, the healthcare industry can enhance patient care, improve outcomes, and drive efficiency, ultimately revolutionizing the way healthcare is delivered.

11

Chapter 11: FinTech: Redefining Financial Services

Financial technology, or FinTech, is disrupting traditional financial services by offering innovative solutions that enhance convenience, efficiency, and accessibility. From mobile banking to blockchain-based platforms, FinTech is reshaping the financial landscape and redefining the way we manage money.

Mobile banking apps provide users with easy access to their accounts, enabling them to perform transactions, check balances, and manage finances from their smartphones. Digital wallets, such as Apple Pay and Google Wallet, offer secure and convenient payment options, reducing the reliance on physical cash and cards.

Blockchain technology is revolutionizing the financial industry by providing a secure and transparent platform for transactions. Smart contracts, powered by blockchain, enable automated and tamper-proof agreements, reducing the need for intermediaries and enhancing trust.

FinTech is also driving financial inclusion by providing access to financial services for underserved populations. Peer-to-peer lending platforms, microfinance solutions, and digital payment systems are empowering individuals and small businesses, promoting economic growth and development.

This chapter explores the rise of FinTech, highlighting key trends, applications, and benefits. By embracing FinTech, businesses can enhance efficiency, improve customer experiences, and drive innovation in the financial sector.

12

Chapter 12: EdTech: Transforming Education

Education technology, or EdTech, is transforming the way we learn and teach, making education more accessible, personalized, and engaging. From online learning platforms to interactive classrooms, EdTech is enhancing the educational experience and preparing students for the challenges of the 21st century.

Online learning platforms, such as Coursera and Khan Academy, provide learners with access to a wide range of courses and educational resources. These platforms offer flexibility and convenience, allowing individuals to learn at their own pace and on their own schedule.

Interactive classrooms equipped with smartboards, tablets, and other digital tools are creating dynamic and immersive learning environments. These technologies facilitate collaboration, creativity, and critical thinking, enhancing student engagement and achievement.

Personalized learning is at the forefront of EdTech, with adaptive learning systems that tailor educational content to individual needs and learning styles. By analyzing student performance data, these systems provide personalized recommendations and support, helping learners achieve their full potential.

13

Chapter 13: The Role of Government and Policy in Tech Innovation

Government policies and regulations play a crucial role in shaping the technology landscape. Supportive policies can foster innovation, while restrictive regulations can hinder progress. This chapter examines the impact of government actions on technological advancements and the importance of creating a favorable environment for innovation.

Governments worldwide are recognizing the potential of technology to drive economic growth and improve quality of life. As a result, they are investing in research and development, providing grants and incentives for tech startups, and creating innovation hubs to nurture new ideas. Public-private partnerships are also gaining prominence, bringing together the resources and expertise of both sectors to accelerate technological progress.

Regulations must balance the need to protect consumers and ensure ethical practices with the need to encourage innovation. For example, data privacy regulations, such as the General Data Protection Regulation (GDPR) in Europe, aim to safeguard personal information while still allowing businesses to harness the power of data. Similarly, regulations governing emerging technologies like AI and autonomous vehicles must ensure safety and accountability without stifling innovation.

Chapter 13: The Role of Government and Policy in Tech...

This chapter explores the role of government and policy in tech innovation, highlighting successful initiatives and best practices from around the world. By creating a supportive regulatory environment and fostering collaboration between the public and private sectors, governments can drive technological progress and create a thriving ecosystem for innovation.

14

Chapter 14: Ethical Considerations in Technology

As technology continues to evolve, ethical considerations become increasingly important. The rapid pace of innovation raises questions about privacy, security, fairness, and accountability. This chapter explores the ethical implications of emerging technologies and the responsibilities of tech pioneers in ensuring their creations are used responsibly.

Data privacy is a significant concern in the digital age, as businesses collect and analyze vast amounts of personal information. Ensuring that data is collected, stored, and used ethically is essential to maintaining trust with consumers. Organizations must be transparent about their data practices and implement robust security measures to protect sensitive information.

Algorithmic bias is another critical issue, particularly in AI and machine learning. Biases in training data can lead to discriminatory outcomes, perpetuating inequalities and harming marginalized communities. Developers must strive to create fair and unbiased algorithms, actively working to identify and mitigate potential biases.

The deployment of autonomous systems, such as self-driving cars and drones, raises questions about accountability and safety. Ensuring that these technologies are designed and implemented with the highest ethical standards

CHAPTER 14: ETHICAL CONSIDERATIONS IN TECHNOLOGY

is essential to preventing harm and building public trust.

This chapter explores the ethical considerations in technology, highlighting the importance of responsible innovation. By prioritizing ethics in their work, tech pioneers can create technologies that benefit society while minimizing potential harms.

15

Chapter 15: The Road Ahead: Embracing Innovation for a Better Future

As we look to the future, the potential trajectories of technological innovation are both exciting and challenging. Businesses must navigate the complexities of the digital age, adapting to new technologies and staying ahead of the curve. This final chapter considers the opportunities and challenges that lie ahead, emphasizing the importance of adaptability and resilience.

Emerging technologies such as quantum computing, biotechnology, and advanced materials hold the promise of transforming industries and solving some of the world's most pressing problems. However, these advancements also come with uncertainties and risks. Businesses must be prepared to navigate these challenges, continuously learning and evolving to remain competitive.

Collaboration and interdisciplinary approaches will be essential to driving innovation. By bringing together diverse perspectives and expertise, businesses can create holistic solutions that address complex issues. Public-private partnerships, open innovation models, and cross-sector collaboration will play a crucial role in shaping the future of technology.

The importance of a forward-thinking mindset cannot be overstated. Embracing change, fostering a culture of innovation, and investing in continuous

CHAPTER 15: THE ROAD AHEAD: EMBRACING INNOVATION FOR A...

learning are essential for businesses to thrive in an ever-changing landscape. By staying agile and resilient, companies can seize new opportunities, drive growth, and contribute to a better future.

Global Tech Pioneers: Unveiling Future Innovations in Business and Beyond

In an era of rapid technological advancement, "Global Tech Pioneers: Unveiling Future Innovations in Business and Beyond" takes you on an enlightening journey through the cutting-edge innovations reshaping our world. This comprehensive guide explores the transformative potential of technologies such as artificial intelligence, blockchain, the Internet of Things, and beyond, highlighting their far-reaching impacts on industries and societies.

From the visionary leaders driving change to the revolutionary applications of emerging technologies, this book delves into the stories and strategies that are redefining the future of business. Each chapter provides in-depth insights into the latest advancements, real-world examples, and practical applications, offering a roadmap for navigating the complexities of the digital age.

Discover how artificial intelligence and machine learning are revolutionizing decision-making, how the Internet of Things is creating a seamlessly connected world, and how blockchain is enhancing security and transparency. Explore the rise of automation and robotics, the power of big data and analytics, and the critical importance of cybersecurity in protecting our digital frontier.

As businesses adapt to digital transformation, this book also examines the future of work, the integration of sustainability and green technology, and the revolutionary impact of HealthTech and FinTech on healthcare and financial services. With a focus on ethical considerations and the role of government and policy in fostering innovation, "Global Tech Pioneers" provides a holistic view of the tech landscape.

Prepare to be inspired by the endless possibilities of technology and the pioneers who are shaping our future. Whether you're a business leader, entrepreneur, or tech enthusiast, this book offers valuable insights and practical guidance for embracing innovation and thriving in the digital age.

www.ingramcontent.com/pod-product-compliance
Lightning Source LLC
LaVergne TN
LVHW010444070526
838199LV00066B/6190